PEARSON
Prentice Hall

Boston, Massachusetts
Upper Saddle River, New Jersey

ISBN 0-13-363639-9

1 2 3 4 5 6 7 8 9 10 11 10 09 08 07

PRENTICE HALL DISCOVERIES

With Our Eyes Open

Do others really see us?

Table of Contents

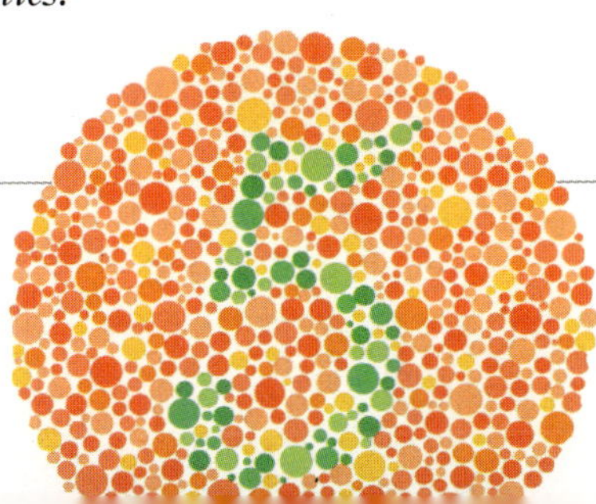

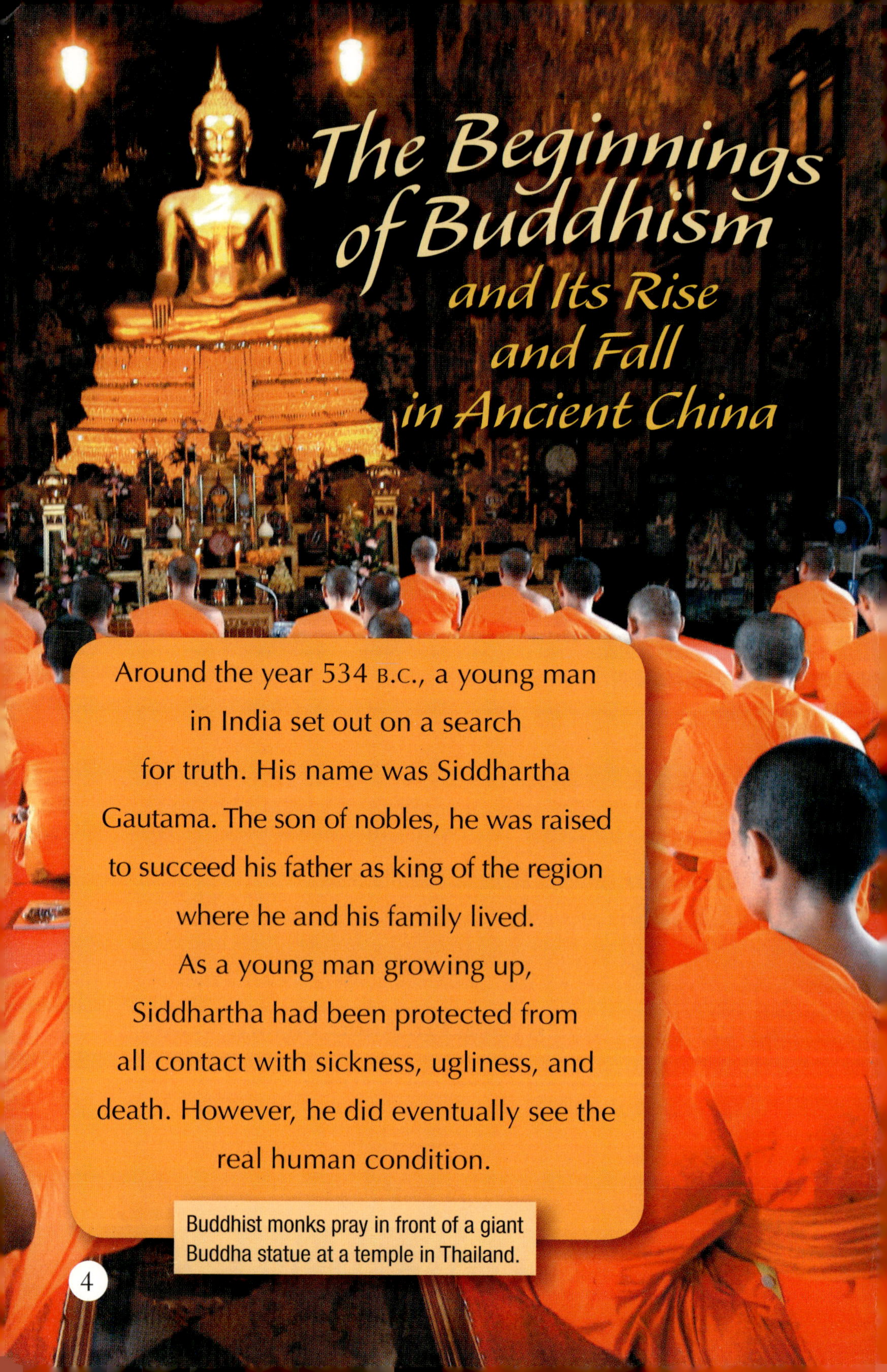

The Beginnings of Buddhism
and Its Rise and Fall in Ancient China

Around the year 534 B.C., a young man in India set out on a search for truth. His name was Siddhartha Gautama. The son of nobles, he was raised to succeed his father as king of the region where he and his family lived.

As a young man growing up, Siddhartha had been protected from all contact with sickness, ugliness, and death. However, he did eventually see the real human condition.

Buddhist monks pray in front of a giant Buddha statue at a temple in Thailand.

SOCIAL STUDIES

Today we know this man as the Buddha, which means "Enlightened One." Buddhism, based on Siddhartha Gautama's teachings, is one of the world's major religions. The Buddha's teachings brought a whole new way of looking at the human experience. Through the ages, followers of those teachings have tried to turn their focus away from self and toward the well-being of humankind.

The Buddha's Life

Because he is so beloved, the Buddha has become larger than life. At times it's hard to sort out what is legend and what is fact when looking at his history. Still, looking at his life, fact and legend, can **contribute** to an understanding of his beliefs.

Childhood and Youth Siddhartha grew up in luxury in the area that is now Nepal. Siddhartha's father did everything he could to keep his son's **focus** on the pleasures of power and wealth. He gave orders that his son could have anything he wanted. He also took great care to make sure Siddhartha would never see the ugly side of life.

By 16, the handsome Siddhartha was married to a beautiful princess. Soon they had a son, Rahula. Siddhartha's life was like a fairy tale, full of beauty and riches. He showed great **potential** for realizing his father's dreams for him of worldly fame and power.

Vocabulary

contribute (kuhn TRIB yoot) *v.* give or share money, knowledge, or ideas

focus (FOH kuhs) *v.* to fix or concentrate on one thing; adjust to make clear

potential (poh TEN shuhl) *n.* possibility; capability

A Time of Change Despite his sheltered life as a young man, legend says that Siddhartha experienced the Four Passing Sights. These encounters changed his life.

The first sight was a **destitute** old man. Legend says that this man had gray, straggly hair and broken teeth. He was bent over, holding onto a tall stick for support. The man was Siddhartha's first encounter with old age.

The next sight was someone suffering from a terrible illness. This was Siddhartha's first experience with disease.

The third sight was a dead body, Siddhartha's first experience with death. Siddhartha's **reaction** to these sights was to conclude that no person could ever escape age, illness, or death. This idea was a shock to him, and he worried about it day and night.

The fourth sight gave Siddhartha a different **perspective**. He encountered a monk. The monk's head was shaved, he wore a simple robe, and he carried

Siddhartha's search for the meaning of life led him to this meeting with a priest.

a bowl for begging. From this encounter, Siddhartha learned about leaving behind worldly needs.

As he became less and less contented with his luxurious and sheltered life, Siddhartha thought more and more about life's true meaning. When he was 29, Siddhartha's **compulsion** to understand the true meaning of life led him to leave his family. He began a search for answers, which would last six years.

Vocabulary

destitute (DES tuh toot) *adj.* living in complete poverty

reaction (ree AK shuhn) *n.* an opposing action; a response

perspective (puhr SPEK tiv) *n.* a specific point of view in understanding or judging things

compulsion (kuhm PUL shuhn) *n.* a driving, irresistible force

The Process of Enlightenment Siddhartha began his search among the holy men of the time. He hoped to **acquire** their wisdom and find answers to his questions. After learning all he could, however, he still did not find the truth he sought.

Siddhartha then moved to live among those who chose to withdraw from the world, living the simplest of lives. He thought that if he controlled his body by denying himself food and comfort, he might see how to escape age and death. These efforts also failed him.

Siddhartha next turned to a life of thought. One evening he sat down under a tree and said he would stay there in a state of deep concentration until the truth was revealed to him. Through 49 days and nights, Siddhartha stayed under that tree. Vision after vision came to him. Then he experienced what he called the Great Awakening. Through that awakening, he found truth. As Siddhartha became the Buddha, the enlightened one, it is said that all living things sang and rejoiced. The whole universe seemed to **appreciate** his greatness.

VOCABULARY

acquire (uh KWYR) *v.* gain possession of

appreciate (uh PREE shee AYT) *v.* be grateful for; recognize worth of something or someone

Siddhartha found truth as he experienced the Great Awakening.

A New Life The Buddha spent the rest of his life traveling throughout India. He spread his message by word of mouth. He set up an order of followers, teaching them what he had learned. Yet every day he took the time for quiet thought, returning in his mind to the source of his beliefs.

The Buddha truly thought it was his mission to guide the world. This wasn't because he was a **conceited** person. He saw this mission as something he was called to do to help others, not something that made him better than other people.

The Buddha's Teachings

Just as the facts of the Buddha's life are fuzzy, the exact details of his teachings aren't always clear. The Buddha did not write his ideas down. Based on the study of others over the centuries since Buddha lived, though, we can **summarize** the foundations of Buddhist beliefs.

Nirvana This is the term for what the Buddha thought of as life's goal. The word *nirvana* means "to blow out" or "to go out," as a candle goes out when there is no longer a wick to burn. People can reach nirvana when they overcome all of their selfish desires and burning emotions. In this way they open themselves to unlimited possibilities. What does that mean? The Buddha himself said that you cannot **define** nirvana.

Four Noble Truths Right after his enlightenment, the Buddha shared what he learned. He called the core ideas the Four Noble Truths.

The First Noble Truth is that life is about suffering. The second Noble Truth explains why. We suffer because we are focused on self. The Third Noble Truth says that when we free ourselves by becoming selfless, we can be happy. This leads to the Fourth Noble Truth, which is a way to create a **void**, or empty place, in the area of selfishness. That way is called the Eightfold Path.

The Eightfold Path The Buddha was a very **practical** person. He did not like to talk about theories. He wanted to solve problems. That is why he presented a way to reach nirvana, or the end to life's problems. The Eightfold Path tells followers how to behave. Followers can see the proper ways to think, speak, act, and work in the world. Someone on this path should never **ignore** the goal, not in any part of life.

Vocabulary

conceited (kuhn SEET id) *adj.* having a very high opinion of oneself

summarize (SUM uh RYZ) *v.* briefly state the most important events in a story

define (dee FYN) *v.* set clear boundaries or distinct characteristics

void (VOYD) *n.* emptiness

practical (PRAK ti kuhl) *adj.* level-headed; efficient; realistic

ignore (ig NOHR) *v.* pay no attention to; refuse to consider; disregard

Buddhist Ideas Spread

By the time the Buddha died at age 80, he and his ideas were widely respected in India. Two centuries later, the Indian King Ashoka wanted to spread Buddhist ideas throughout the kingdom. Buddha's followers, the monks, were encouraged to travel far and wide teaching all Indian people about Buddhism.

Soon some rulers of neighboring kingdoms also became Buddhists. The **involvement** of such powerful people helped to hasten the spread of ideas. Then, when the Silk Road opened around the second century B.C., it provided a way for Buddhist ideas to spread even farther. People began traveling between India, central Asia, and China, taking their ideas as well as their goods with them.

Buddhist ideas began to spread as people traveled the Silk Road.

The golden Buddha

Buddhism Spreads to China Legend says that in A.D. 68 the Han emperor in China had a dream about a golden Buddha. He sent a trusted man to India to learn more about Buddhist ideas. Three years later the man returned to China with Buddhist writings, art, and two Buddhist monks. From that point on, Buddhism had a strong foothold in China. By around A.D. 514, two million Buddhists lived in China.

Vocabulary

involvement (in VAHLV muhnt)) *n.* participation

Confucius

Why did Buddhism have such a strong following in China? One reason is that it fit well with existing Chinese beliefs, especially Confucianism. Confucius was a wise man who lived in China from 551 to 479 B.C. He believed in the importance of tradition and family. He believed that people should behave in orderly ways. Confucius taught that all goodness begins in the home. Confucianism says that honesty, courage, courtesy, and truthfulness are what people should **emphasize** in raising their children.

Confucius was not interested in religion. He was interested in teaching people how to live wisely. This is not in **conflict** with the ideas of Buddhism. The Buddha also was interested in helping people to live in the right way. People could follow both systems at the same time.

Buddhism also appealed to people who were weary of the turmoil in China. For nearly three hundred years after the Han dynasty fell in A.D. 220, China was not unified. In the face of constant change and fighting, many Chinese people were drawn to Buddhist ideas. After so much fighting, they could appreciate a path that would lead to inner peace.

The Tang Dynasty: The Height of Chinese Buddhism

When the Tang dynasty came to power in A.D. 618, many say China's greatest period began. This golden age of power, wealth, and culture is still a source of **pride** among Chinese people.

Under the Tang dynasty, China was once again unified. The empire spread, becoming the greatest power in Asia. Most of the Tang emperors ruled with **benevolence**, seeking peace and stability. Every male head of a family was given land. The smartest people, rather than the richest or most powerful, were given authority in the government.

The Impact on the Arts Another strong **characteristic** of Tang rulers was their openness to new ideas. The great cities of China drew people from faraway lands. Their different views and ways of life were welcome in Tang China. Music, art, literature, sports, religion—all of these areas developed in new ways because of the impact of many cultures.

Vocabulary

emphasize (EM fuh syz) *v.* stress something in order to make it stand out

conflict (KAHN flikt) *n.* opposition between or among different forces; clash

pride (PRYD) *n.* proper respect for yourself; sense of your own dignity or worth; self-respect

benevolence (buh NEV uh luhns) *n.* kindliness

characteristic (KAR uhk tuhr IS tik) *n.* a quality that makes something recognizable

Tang Rulers and Buddhist Influence During the first half of the Tang dynasty, several rulers were supporters of Buddhist beliefs. They openly gave land and money to Buddhist monks and scholars. In turn, the Buddhists honored the rulers.

The reign of China's only empress might best **illustrate** how Buddhists and rulers helped to further each other's interests. Empress Wu Chao probably would not have come into power without the help of Buddhists. They believed that she was an important Buddhist savior who had come back to life. Therefore, they lent her all of their support. Once she was in power, Empress Wu Chao's open commitment to Buddhist beliefs was able to **arouse** the interest of millions of Chinese. More followers meant more power and money for those who followed Buddhism.

Empress Wu Chao ruled China from 690 to 705.

As the Tang dynasty continued to grow in wealth and power, so did Buddhism. Similarly, when the dynasty began to decline, many of the ideas that had flourished fell out of favor. This would be true of Buddhism.

Why Buddhism Declined in China

The turning point in Tang China occurred in A.D. 755. This is when a powerful general led a rebellion against the dynasty. The emperor had to flee, which caused people to view the system as weak. Although the dynasty continued until A.D. 907, it was never the same.

During this period of decline, leaders began to criticize the new belief systems in China. Many felt that power in China had been given to too many foreigners. They were especially angry about the wealth and power of Buddhists.

The Silent Religion In A.D. 845, the Tang dynasty took actions to eliminate Buddhism. In that year, tens of thousands of Buddhist buildings were destroyed. Many Buddhist leaders were forced out. As the golden age of China drew to a close, Buddhism was forced underground. It would live on but as a silent religion. In the future, Buddhism also would be much less unified, as groups throughout Asia began to practice the beliefs in very different ways.

In contrast, Confucianism surged during the second half of the Tang dynasty. With its basis in traditional Chinese beliefs, it was viewed very favorably. All leaders were expected to govern as Confucius had taught.

Vocabulary

illustrate (IL uh STRAYT) *v.* make clear or easily understood by examples

arouse (uh ROWZ) *v.* awaken one's attention or interest; stir into action

Tang Buddhism Lives on in Art and Literature

Often when a society prospers, the arts also blossom. When people's needs for food, shelter, and safety are met, they can take time to look for and create beauty.

In the Tang dynasty, music, art, and literature all flourished. In all art forms the blending of cultures can be seen.

Longquan temple in China

Buddhism and Art and Architecture Buddhist influences are especially apparent in Tang arts. Sculptors created faces like those of India. A western style of painting, using a thick line to outline figures, was used on paintings that adorned many Chinese Buddhist temples. The temples and other buildings were also built with a blended style that came to be known as Buddhist architecture.

Buddhism and Literature In literature, the Tang era was centered on poetry. Tens of thousands of poems were written and saved. As any **critique** of poems from this period will tell you, Buddhist thought was a major influence. Many of the poems celebrate a simple life lived amid nature. Some of the greatest poets, including Wang Wei, were very important in Chinese government. They often chose to **respond** to the glory of life at court by taking long rests in

Vocabulary

critique (kri TEEK) *n.* an assessment or critical analysis, usually of a creative or literary work

respond (ree SPAHND) *v.* to reply or act in answering

the country. There they would try to escape the world and themselves, seeking peace. They would write while emptying their minds of daily cares.

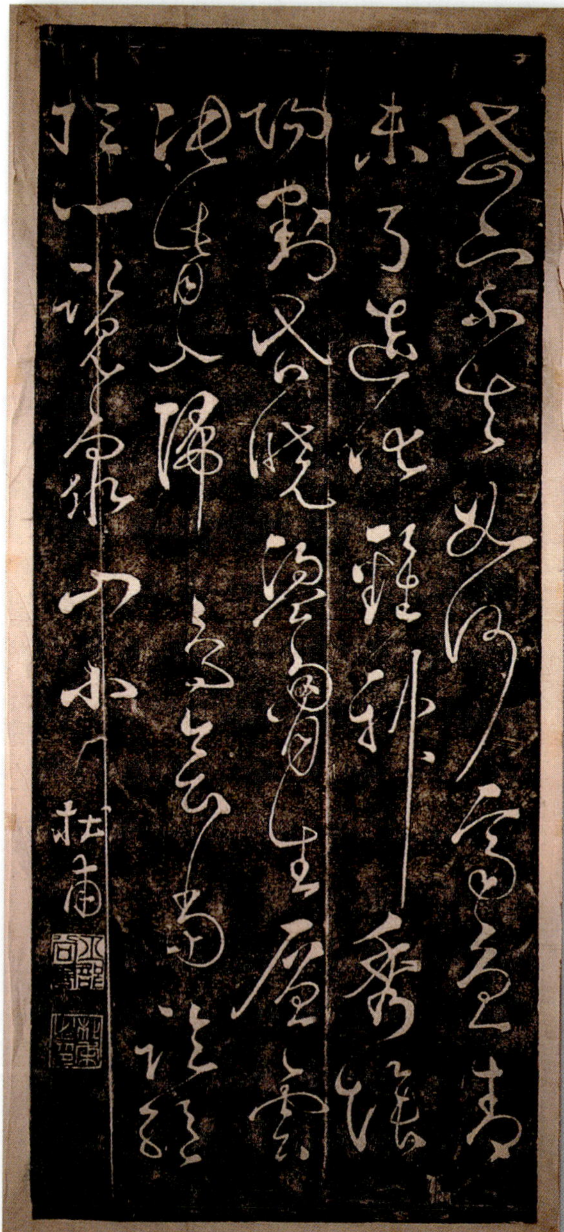

This rubbing is from a stone with a carved surface. Much of China's history and literature was recorded on these stones during the Tang dynasty.

Thus, Tang poems give us a glimpse into how Buddhists long ago saw the world while balancing these views with worldly success. The Buddha's influence continues to this day, influencing the way people see themselves, see others, and see the world.

Discussion Questions

1. Siddhartha Gautama was shocked and confused the first time he saw human suffering. After he became the Buddha, how do you think he reacted when he saw someone suffering? How do you think the sight of suffering makes most people feel?

2. Do you think it is actually possible, or even good, to think of yourself much less often than you think of others? Why or why not?

3. What do you think pieces of art, music, and literature can tell us about the culture of the people who created them? Why is it important to study these aspects of ancient cultures as well as the facts about what happened long ago?

Now You See It!

VISION

Vision is one of our most important senses. Our eyesight works as the result of the connection between our eyes and the brain. Vision gives us pleasure, and it warns us of danger. It allows us to perform endless activities, and it enables us to perceive our surroundings and the people around us. How does our vision work? Do we all see the same thing when we look at something? What is colorblindness? What causes optical **illusions**? Is seeing really believing? Let's find out.

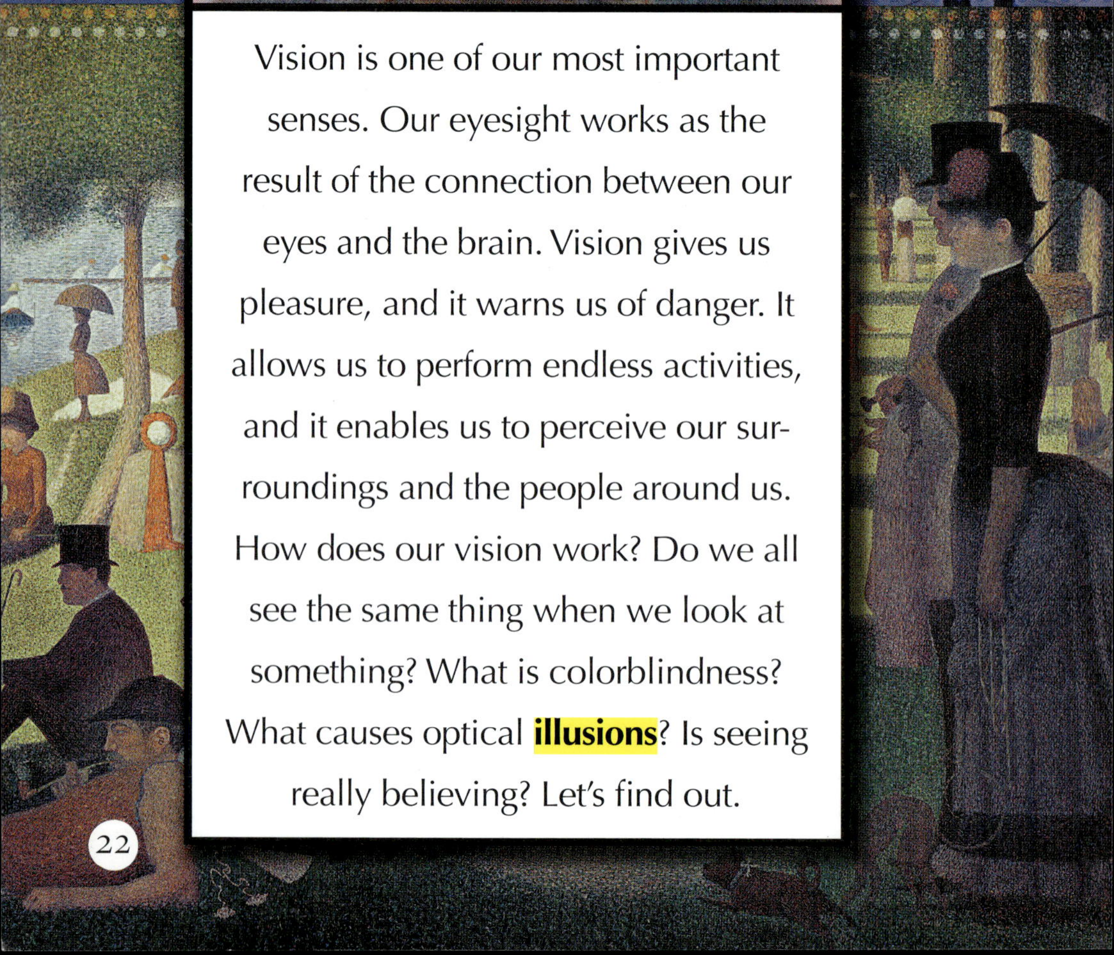

The Amazing Eye

Our eyes are constantly busy seeing images and sending them to our brains where they are recognized and understood. How does this astounding process take place? To **appreciate** how our vision works, we need to take a close look at the eye's structure.

Eyeball Each of your two eyeballs is a small round ball that sits in an opening called an eye socket. An eyeball is about one inch across, about the size of a ping-pong ball. You cannot see your entire eyeball because your eyelids cover part of it. Eyelids protect the eye and help keep the eye wet with tears.

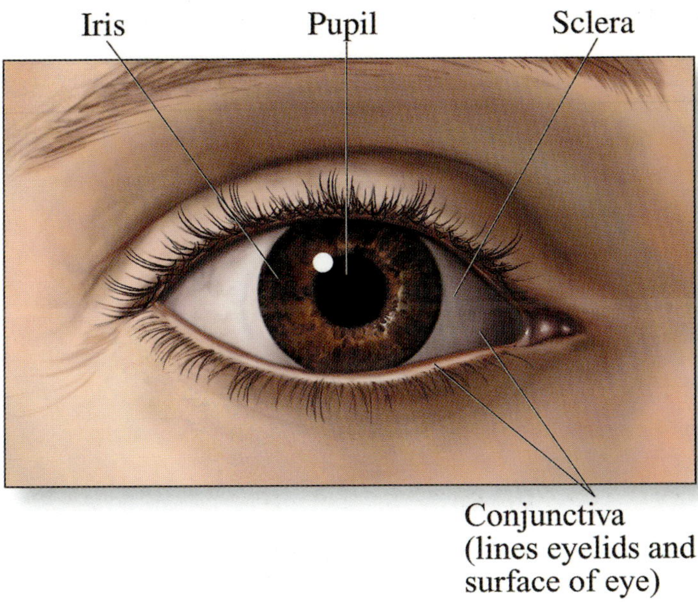

Vocabulary

illusion (i LOO zhun) *n.* an unreal, deceptive, or misleading appearance or image

appreciate (uh PREE shee AYT) *v.* be grateful for; recognize worth of something or someone

SCIENCE

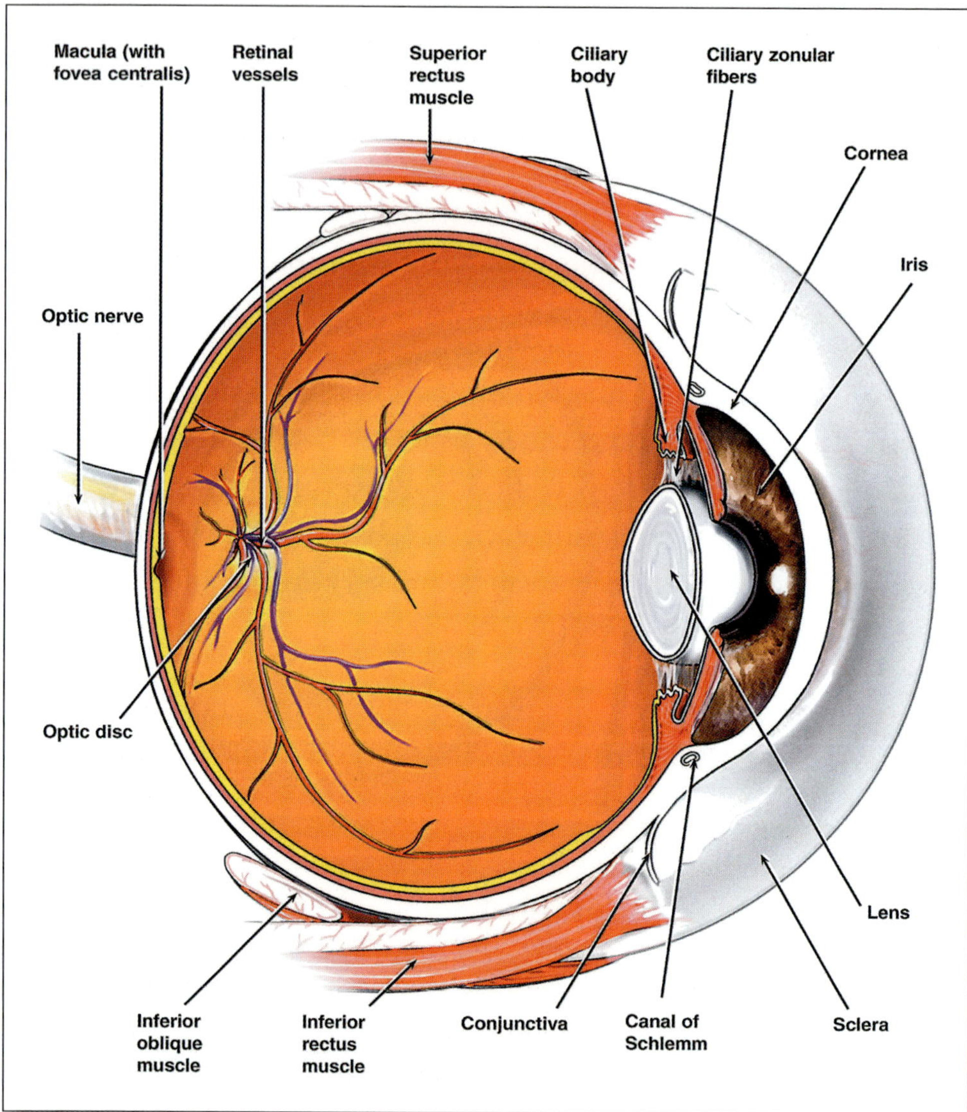

Structure of the human eye

Eye Muscles The eyeball is held in place by eye muscles. These six very tiny muscles are important because they also control the way the eyeball moves in its socket. Think of the many directions in which your eyes can move. They can move up and down, from side to side, and at an angle up and away from your face, as well as down and away. These movements help us "keep an eye" on our surroundings. That way we avoid **potential** danger as we navigate our way through the world.

Cornea The cornea is the clear layer in front of the eyeball. Light enters the eye through the cornea. The cornea is often compared to a camera lens because it bends light as it enters the eyeball. Right behind the cornea is a clear liquid called the *aqueous humor.*

Pupil The pupil is behind the cornea. It is the black part of your eye. It is really an open hole through which light passes.

Iris and Sclera The iris is the colored part of your eye. The white of your eye is the sclera. Strong muscles in the iris control the size of your pupil. If there is a lot of light, the iris will **respond** and make the pupil smaller. In the dark, the pupil becomes larger to let in more light.

Lens Right behind the pupil lies the lens. It looks like a jelly-filled vitamin capsule. The lens's **involvement** in the process of seeing is vital. Its job, like the cornea, is to **focus** the light that enters the eye. The lens is different from the cornea, however, because it is able to change

Vocabulary

potential (poh TEN shuhl) *adj.* possible; that can, but has not yet, come into being

respond (ree SPAHND) *v.* to reply or act in answering

involvement (in VAHLV muhnt)) *n.* participation

focus (FOH kuhs) *v.* to fix or concentrate on one thing; adjust to make clear

shape in order to focus clearly on objects. When you look at a faraway object, the lens becomes flatter and thinner. The shape of the lens bulges out when you look at something that is close by. Behind the lens is a round pocket of clear liquid called the *vitreous humor.* This liquid gives the eyeball its round shape.

Retina and Optic Nerve The layer of cells at the back of the eye is called the retina. After light passes through the vitreous humor, it is focused on the retina. The special light-sensitive cells in the retina change the light into nerve impulses. These nerve impulses are sent along the optic nerve, which is at the back of the eye and travels to the brain. These impulses are the "messages" that the brain receives as the images that we see.

How Do We See?

Your eyes and their connection to your brain give you vision. Let's **summarize** the **sequence** of events that happens every time you look at something. To make the order of these events clearer, pretend that you are looking at a house. First of all, remember that there is usually light all around us. Sources of light include the sun or artificial light that comes from an electric light bulb.

Light is constantly hitting the objects around you. Then, the light bounces off the objects. Scientists say the light is reflected off the objects. In the case of the house you are looking at, light hits it and is reflected off it. That reflected light enters your eye. It passes through the cornea and then through the aqueous humor. Next it passes through your pupil and then through the lens and vitreous humor. The lens forms an upside-down **image** of the house on the retina, at the back of your eyeball. The retina passes the image, in the form of nerve impulses, to the optic nerve. From there, the image travels to the brain and is turned into a right-side up picture. That picture is understood by your brain to be an image of a house.

Vocabulary

summarize (SUM uh RYZ) *v.* briefly state the most important events in a story

sequence (SEE kwuhns) *n.* one thing after another in logical or chronological order

image (IM ij) *n.* picture

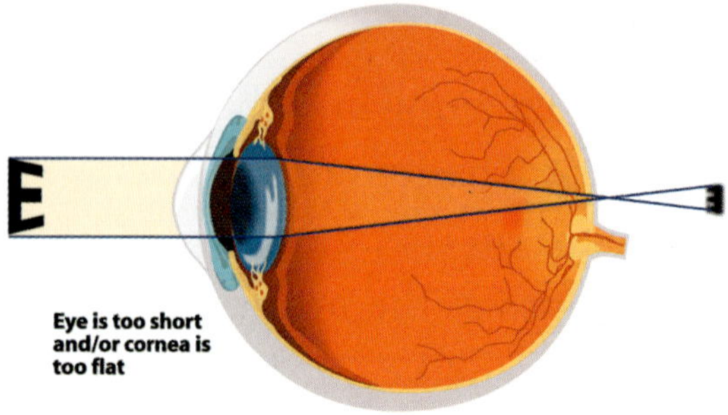

The top diagram shows where an image forms in hyperopia.
The bottom diagram shows where an image forms in myopia.

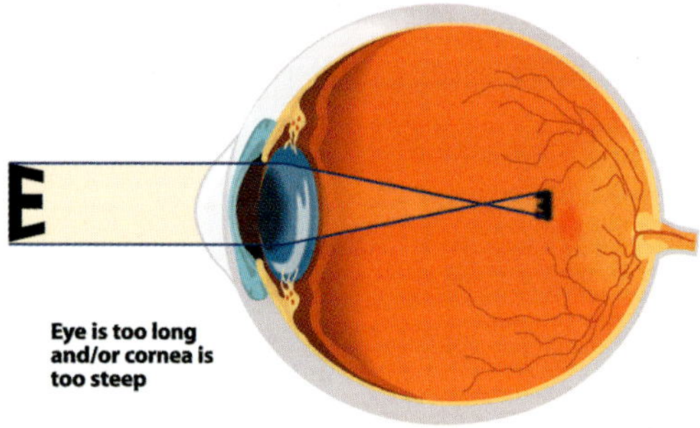

Not all eyes have normal vision. Look at the diagrams on this page. They **illustrate** where the image of an E appears when someone does not have normal vision. In one case, the image is outside the scope of the eyeball. This happens because the eyeball's shape is longer from top to bottom. This is called farsighted vision, or *hyperopia.* Farsighted people can see things that are far away clearly, but have trouble seeing close-up objects.

The other illustration shows someone with nearsighted vision, or *myopia.* In that case, the person can see close-up objects well, but has difficulty seeing faraway things. Again, this is due to the shape of the eyeball, which is wider than normal from back to front. This causes the image of the E to fall short of the retina.

Eye tests can determine cases of near- and farsightedness, and these conditions can be corrected with eyeglasses or contact lenses.

Why Do We Have Two Eyes?

Two eyes are better than one for a couple of reasons. First, if one eye is injured or blinded, the other eye is ready to serve as a backup, and vision is not lost.

The second reason we have two eyes is because they work together to give us *depth* **perception**. Scientists **define** depth perception as seeing in three dimensions. We use depth perception to judge how far away from us an object is. Depth perception allows us to pour a glass of milk without spilling a drop. It enables us to swing a bat at a ball and hit it. It is also very important for jobs that require a lot of hand-eye coordination, such as setting jewels or performing surgery.

Vocabulary

illustrate (IL uh STRAYT) *v.* make clear or easily understood by examples

perception (puhr SEP shuhn) *n.* ability to see

define (dee FYN) *v.* set clear boundaries or distinct characteristics

Depth perception lets you judge how far away a train is.

Depth perception results when the images sent to your brain by both eyes are blended together. This is called *fusion.* There is an easy way to see how depth perception works. Cover one eye and look at an object. The object's position seems to shift a bit. Then look at the same object while covering the other eye. Once again the image shifts a bit. If you reach out to touch the object, your aim will be off a little. Now look at the object with both eyes. It comes into focus, and you are able to judge its exact location. It may **astonish** you to know that the brain is able to keep the images blended into one image, even though your eyes are constantly moving and changing direction as you gaze at the object!

How Do We See Colors?

Do you have a favorite color? The world would certainly be a drabber place without it. Colors **contribute** much of the visual enjoyment we get from our surroundings. Colors have the power to **arouse** our emotions and to affect our moods. Each time we look at a clear blue sky, a yellow rose, a bright red cardinal, or the color of a favorite shirt, we respond to the beauty of colors.

Color vision involves the retina. Two kinds of cells are found in the retina. They are called *rods* and *cones.* There are over one million rods and about six million cones in each retina. Rods are highly sensitive to light and help you to see in dim light. They do not perceive colors, however. Rods allow you to see in tones of black, white, and gray. At night, when there is not much light, the rods in your eyes let you see. Cones, on the other hand, help you see fine detail and colors, but they do not function in dim light. To see colors, we therefore must have light.

Vocabulary

astonish (uh STON ish) *v.* amaze

contribute (kuhn TRIB yoot) *v.* give or share money, knowledge, or ideas

arouse (uh ROWZ) *v.* awaken one's attention or interest; stir into action

This is a microscopic picture of the eye's retina. Rods are shown in brown, and cones are shown in green.

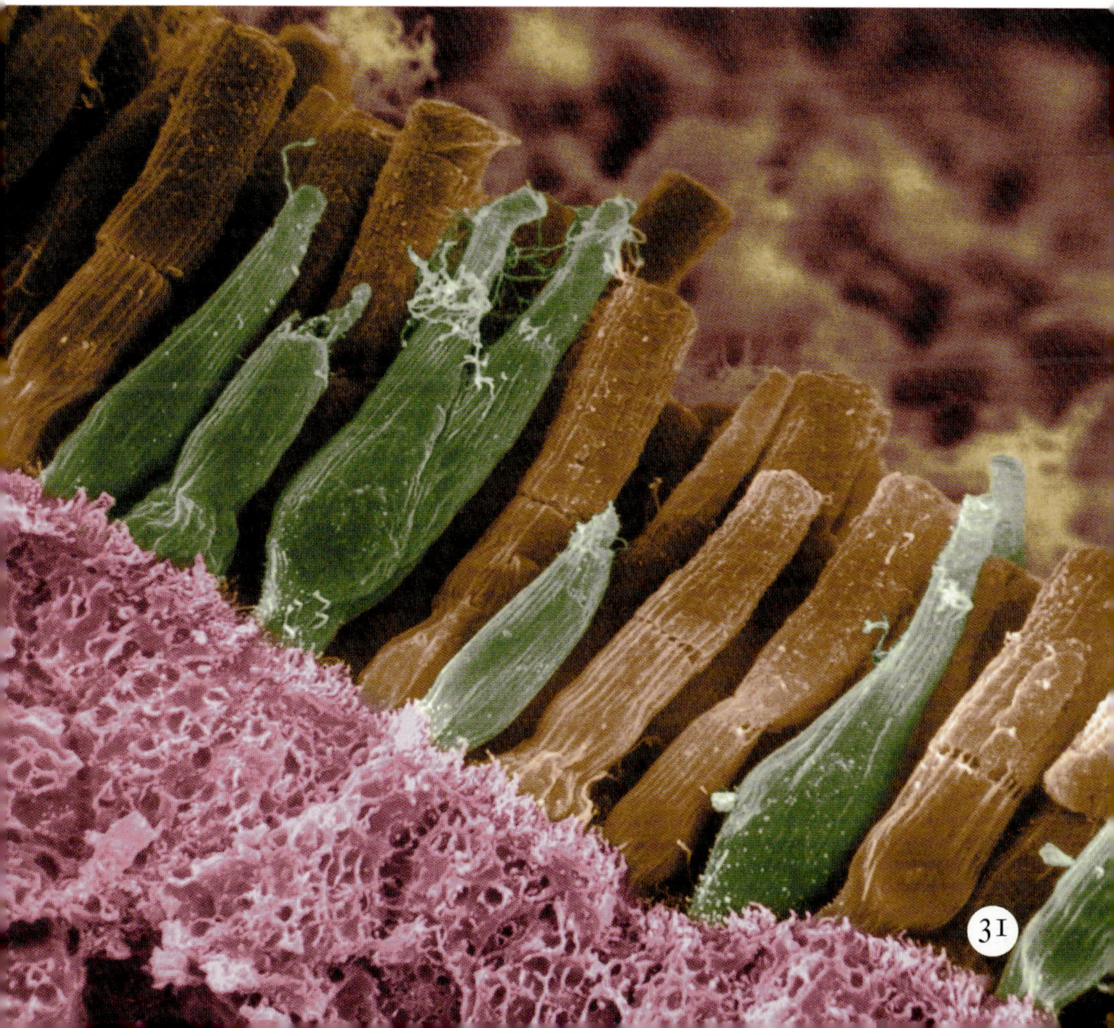

Did you know that we have a *blind spot* in each of our eyes? It is found on the retina where it connects to the optic nerve. In that spot there are no cones or rods, so the retina cannot **establish** an image there. We usually are not aware of this small blind spot because our eyes are moving at all times, so our brains are still receiving images. We also have two eyes sending images to the brain, so even if one eye experiences a blind spot, the other eye does not.

What Is Colorblindness?

Colorblindness is a condition in which the retina's cone cells do not work properly. Normal cones are sensitive to color: some respond to shades of green, some are sensitive to red, and others sense shades of blue. Colorblind people have trouble distinguishing some or all colors. In true colorblindness, called *achromatopsia,* the cones do not work at all, and the person cannot see any colors, only black, white, and gray. Other types of colorblindness, or color deficiency, affect a person's inability to tell red and green apart. Red/green colorblindness is the most common type of color deficiency. The inability to tell blue and yellow apart is a **characteristic** of a less common type of color deficiency.

Most people who are colorblind are born with the condition, and it cannot be cured. Others may **acquire** colorblindness as a **reaction** to a medication or as a side effect of another disease. Men make up more than 90 percent of all colorblind people.

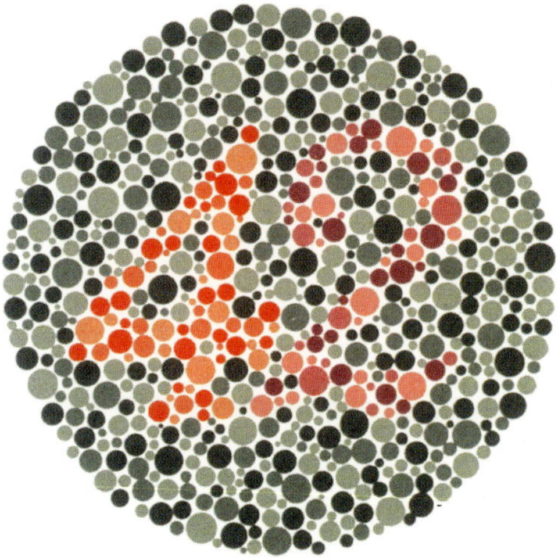 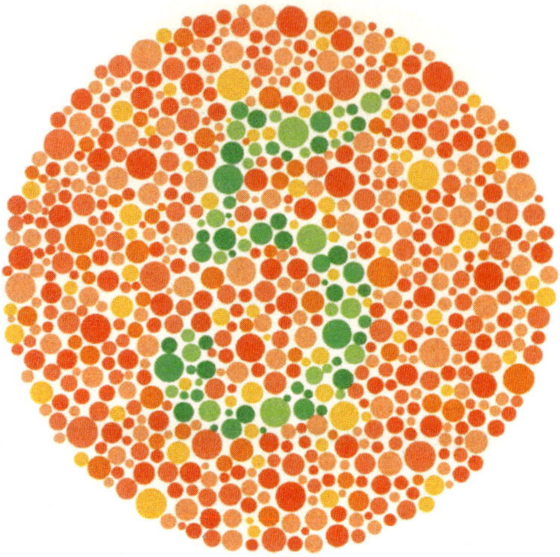

People with red-green color blindness cannot see the number 42 in the left circle or the number 5 in the right circle.

There are tests to determine colorblindness. The most frequently used tests are designed to find red/green colorblindness. Such tests show images of red and green dots. The pattern of the red dots may form a picture of a number or letter upon a field of green dots. A color-blind person will not be able to see the picture because he or she cannot distinguish the red from the green dots. Other tests for colorblindness **involve** identifying and grouping different samples of color shades.

Vocabulary

establish (uh STAB lish) *v.* determine; make sure of; set up

characteristic (KAR uhk tuhr IS tik) *n.* a quality that makes something recognizable

acquire (uh KWYR) *v.* gain possession of

reaction (ree AK shuhn) *n.* an opposing action; a response

involve (in VAHLV) *v.* include in an activity, discussion, or task; make complicated

Hint: Look at the girl's necklace. It's the old woman's mouth. The girl's ear is the old woman's eye.

What Are Optical Illusions?

Have you ever heard the expression "seeing is believing"? We constantly make the **assumption** that what we are seeing is proof that it is real. Most of the time we are right to **conclude** this. Optical illusions, however, are an exception to the rule. These images trick our eyes and brain and fool us into thinking we are seeing something that is not really there.

Look at the optical illusions on these pages. Did they fool you? If so, here is how it happened. Scientists are still discovering how the brain works, but they do know that it is not designed to work slowly and **sluggishly**,

How many ducks do you see in this drawing? Which direction are they flying?

Vocabulary

assumption (uh SUMP shuhn) *n.* the act of assuming or taking for granted

conclude (kuhn KLOOD) *v.* form an opinion based on evidence

sluggishly (SLUG ish lee) *adv.* as if lacking energy

but at astonishing speed. These tricks of the eyes and brain happen when the brain's quick-working memory takes a "short cut" and fills in the details of what you are seeing—even though those details are not really there. Your memory is built on past experiences and upon things with which you are familiar. When seeing something unfamiliar, your brain has a **meager** number of memories that relate to the image. The brain may try to make sense of it by using memories of familiar images. It may **emphasize** some details and ignore others. Sometimes that results in you thinking you are seeing something that isn't really there.

Vocabulary

meager (MEE ger) *adj.* of poor quality; small amount

emphasize (EM fuh syz) *v.* stress something in order to make it stand out

This painting by Maurits Escher shows a waterfall that could not possibly exist.

Many people have their sight tested using a device that contains different lenses.

Our Amazing Eyesight

Vision is one of the marvels of the human body because it allows us to see our world. The way our eyes and brain work together to accomplish this feat is fascinating. The next time you see a beautiful sunset or watch a movie or look at a friend, think of all that is going on in your body in order to view that sight. You're certain "to see" it's amazing!

Discussion Questions

1. There is a figure of speech that says "a picture is worth a thousand words." What do you think this means? Do you agree with this expression? Why or why not?

2. Scientists have found that people pick up other people's moods and feelings by looking at someone's face. This happens all the time when two people are speaking face to face. When people communicate on the computer without a camera, they cannot see each other. Do you think this affects the way they talk to each other? Why or why not? If so, in what ways does it affect communication?

3. Many metaphors and figures of speech are based on words about our eyes and our sense of sight. Some examples are:
   It's an eyeful!
   Do you see what I mean?
   Get the picture?

   Think of some expressions that are based on eyes or our sight, and write them down. What do they mean? Why do you think such expressions came into being?

Screaming in the Dark:

Monsters at the Movies

Can we ever really know another person? We can pile up a mountain of ideas about others, but some mystery always remains. And that mystery can be frightening. From one point of view, monster movies reflect our fears about other people. They can also reflect deep fears about ourselves and our world.

Monsters have been in the movies almost as long as there have been movies. The first real movies were shown by the Lumiere brothers in Paris in 1895. Just one year later, the director Georges Méliès was already **astonishing** audiences. He presented a shocking parade of movie monsters in his short film, *The Devil's Castle.* In just three minutes, the audience witnessed ghosts, skeletons, and witches. Since then, monsters have been the leading characters in some of the most popular movies ever made.

Although many people view movies on television, monster movies are often more effective with a large, live audience in a movie theater. Part of the fun is being **involved**. When the monster suddenly appears, the audience's **reaction** is contagious. Screams ring in the dark as the audience confronts a pure burst of fear.

Vocabulary

reflect (ri FLEKT) *v.* express; show

astonish (uh STON ish) *v.* amaze

involve (in VAHLV) *v.* include in an activity, discussion, or task; make complicated

reaction (ree AK shuhn) *n.* an opposing action; a response

Alarming Changes

When everything stays the same, we feel comfortable. Surprises can be scary. Of course, surprises are also unavoidable. We can't control everything. Some movie monsters **focus** on our fear of sudden, dramatic changes. People who seem normal or average suddenly transform into ghastly creatures.

There have been many movie versions of *Dr. Jekyll and Mr. Hyde,* based on a novel by Robert Louis Stevenson. Dr. Jekyll experiments with a potion to try to purify the human spirit. Instead, he turns into Mr. Hyde, a physical embodiment of his evil side. In the earliest versions, Mr. Hyde looked like an ape man, hairy and savage. In 1920, Lionel Barrymore's make-up **emphasized** Mr. Hyde's reptilian nature. He had spidery limbs and a pointed head.

Werewolf movies tease audiences with the **metamorphosis** of a human into a wolf. *An American Werewolf in London* (1981) brought new attention to this classic theme. The **sequence** of events is familiar. First, a tourist is bitten by a werewolf. Then, when the moon is full, he transforms into a wild animal with a taste for blood. Like many more recent monster movies, this film combines humor with horror. Realistic special effects add to the mix.

In David Cronenberg's remake of 1958's *The Fly,* the fearful change is from human to insect. In a lab accident, a scientist's genetic material is accidentally combined with a fly. A **compulsion** to eat sugar is just the first sign of his transformation into a half-fly, half-human monster.

Some movies have used monstrous makeovers as a metaphor for teenage anxiety. After all, adolescence is a natural change that no one can control. Movies like *I Was a Teenage Werewolf* (1957), *Carrie* (1976), and *Ginger Snaps* (2000) have **conveyed** the frightening changes of adolescence in shockingly literal terms.

Vocabulary

focus (FOH kuhs) *v.* to fix or concentrate on one thing; adjust to make clear

emphasize (EM fuh syz) *v.* stress something in order to make it stand out

metamorphosis (MET uh MOHR fuh sis) *n.* change of form

sequence (SEE kwuhns) *n.* one thing after another in logical or chronological order

compulsion (kuhm PUL shuhn) *n.* a driving, irresistible force

conveyed (kuhn VAYD) *v.* made known; expressed

The 1941 movie *The Wolf Man* starred Lon Chaney, Jr., as a man who transforms into a werewolf. It was the first horror movie about werewolves.

Made in 1931, *Dracula* was the first horror film with sound.

The Dead Are Alive

Fear of death is another basic human emotion. Many movies have **responded** to this fear. They present monsters that blur the line between life and death. Mary Shelley's classic novel *Frankenstein* has inspired dozens of films. Dr. Frankenstein's **defiant** attempt to challenge death leads to tragedy. Using parts from dead bodies, he brings his creature to life. Inevitably, he then loses control of the monster. The message is clear: Frankenstein pays a high price for **ignoring** the natural laws of life, and death is dangerous business.

Other classic film characters such as Dracula and the Mummy also walk this dangerous line. Vampires are also known as the undead. They can be **defined** as people who have died but still exist. Therefore, they cannot die again. The Mummy is an ancient Egyptian corpse brought back to life.

Some monster movies are haunted by ghosts, spirits from another world. Contemporary directors have uncovered ghosts in the technology we use every day. In Steven Spielberg's *Poltergeist* (1982), a television set becomes the connection through which troubled spirits enter a modern suburban world. The 1998 Japanese film *Ringu* (and its 2002 American remake, *The Ring*) imagines an angry ghost that kills anyone who views a haunted videotape.

Zombies are bodies brought back to life, without a soul. *The Night of the Living Dead* (1968) **aroused** fear in audiences across the country. Its realistic **conflict** between innocent people and flesh-eating zombies inspired many horror movies. In 2004, *Shaun of the Dead* found comic new life in the zombie genre.

Vocabulary

respond (ree SPAHND) *v.* to reply or act in answering

defiant (dee FY uhnt) *adj.* boldly resisting

ignore (ig NOHR) *v.* pay no attention to; refuse to consider; disregard

define (dee FYN) *v.* set clear boundaries or distinct characteristics

arouse (uh ROWZ) *v.* awaken one's attention or interest; stir into action

conflict (KAHN flikt) *n.* opposition between or among different forces, clash

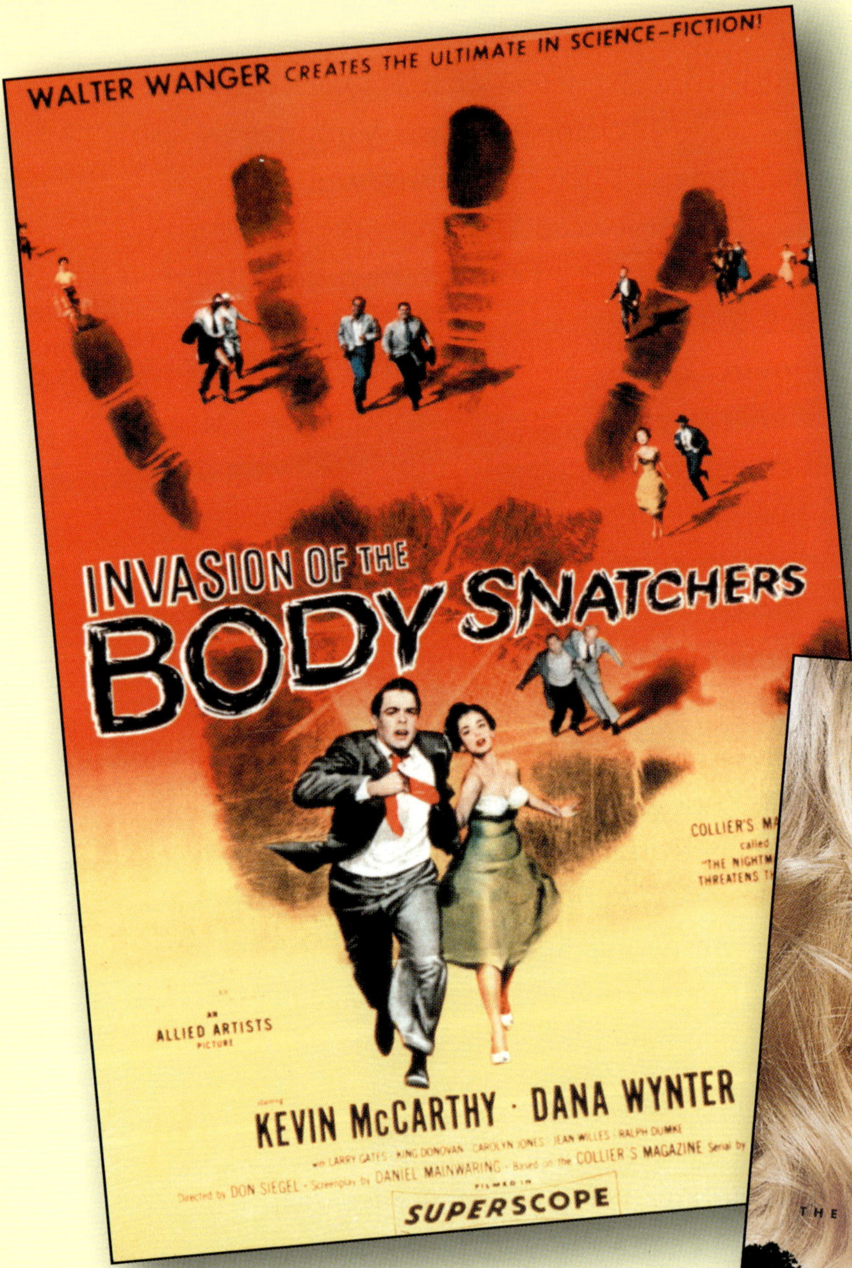

In *Invasion of the Body Snatchers,* human bodies were taken over by "plant pods" from outer space.

In *The Stepford Wives,* a woman notices very strange behavior in her too-perfect female neighbors.

The Human Horror

In some monster movies, the horror is within our own bodies. Body parts develop a mind of their own. In *The Beast with Five Fingers* (1946), the monster is a severed hand. The title pretty much defines the monsters in *The Crawling Eye* (1958). Brains creep and kill in *The Fiend Without a Face* (1957).

The human body itself can become monstrous when it is enlarged. A plutonium explosion in *The Amazing Colossal Man* (1957) has a surprising effect on a soldier. As a result, he grows ten feet a day. A similarly gigantic woman went on a rampage in 1958's *The Attack of the 50-Foot Woman.*

Other films find horror in the idea of losing control over one's own body. In both *The Thing* (1951) and *Invasion of the Body Snatchers* (1955), aliens move into people's bodies. The human characters must find ways to **identify** aliens hiding within their human hosts. In *The Stepford Wives* (1974 and 2004), suburban women are replaced with robots. David Cronenberg's *Scanners* (1980) involves people who are able to tap into other people's nervous systems. These "scanners" can control other people's actions and cause pain.

Vocabulary

identify (eye DEN tuh fy) *v.* recognize something or discover exactly what it is

Creepy, Crawly Things

Of course, not all monsters are based on humans. In fact, many of the most terrifying monsters aren't human at all. Creature designers draw on images from mythology, legends, and nightmares. Their monsters are fierce and horrible beasts.

Monsters from the Animal Kingdom Monster movies can play with our fear of dangerous animals. Truly deadly animals, like the man-eating sharks in *Jaws* (1975) and *Open Water* (2003), can be presented almost realistically. Other movies exaggerate an animal's size or powers to make them extra scary. Three versions of *King Kong* (1933, 1976, and 2005) have scared audiences with a giant ape. *Anaconda* (1997) features a jumbo deadly snake. In *Cujo* (1983), a bat bite turns a cuddly St. Bernard into a deadly killer.

Other movies make animals scarier by adding more of them. If one rat makes your skin crawl, how about an army of thousands of them? *Willard* (1971 and 2003) focuses on a lonely man who can control a squirming sea of rats. Other ghastly groups storm through *The Birds* (1963), *Frogs* (1972), and *The Swarm* (1978, killer bees). In *Snakes on a Plane* (2006), airline passengers are quite flustered when a box of deadly snakes is let loose.

Of course, some movies use both tactics. They make the animals bigger and then add lots of them. Giant ants stalk humans in *Them* (1954). In *Eight Legged Freaks* (2002), radiation causes countless spiders to grow huge and attack.

People found the great white shark in *Jaws* so scary that they stayed away from beaches during the summer of 1975.

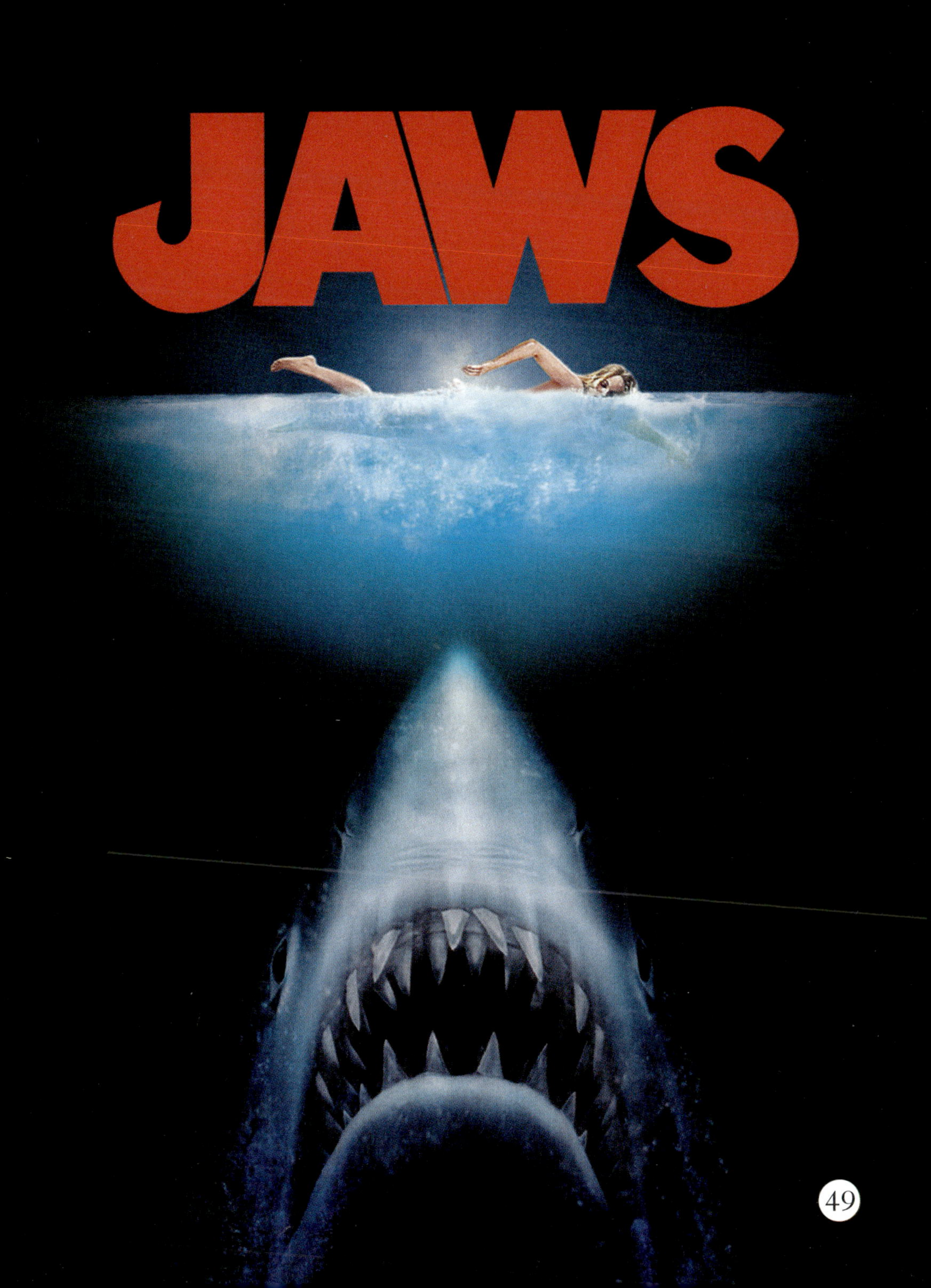

Extinct But Not Forgotten Dinosaurs may be extinct in real life, but they are still alive in many monster movies. Looked at in **chronological** order, dinosaur films emphasize remarkable changes in special effects technology. *Godzilla* (1955) shows a prehistoric monster that terrorizes Tokyo, **snuffing** out dozens of unlucky victims. Today, the most obvious **characteristic** of this monster is that it looks a lot like a man in a rubber suit. Even less convincing, the "dinosaurs" in 1960's *The Lost World* were played by real reptiles. Their dinosaur fins were taped on.

In 1993, Steven Spielberg's *Jurassic Park* used computer graphics to bring dinosaurs back to life. This film **established** a new level of realism in monster movies. Skin textures look authentic. Details are based on careful research. Even the **audible** noises that the dinosaurs make seem genuine. A 1998 remake of *Godzilla* used these new techniques to recreate Japan's famous stalker. The results were realistic, but lacked some of the charm of the admittedly fake-looking original.

Vocabulary

chronological (KRAHN uh LAHJ I kuhl) *adj.* arranged in the order in which events occur

snuffs (SNUFS) *v.* extinguishes; puts out

characteristic (KAR uhk tuhr IS tik) *n.* a quality that makes something recognizable

establish (uh STAB lish) *v.* determine; make sure of; set up

audible (AW duh buhl) *adj.* loud enough to be heard

In the first *Godzilla* movie, atomic tests awakened a prehistoric dinosaur, which then went on a rampage, burning Tokyo to the ground with its breath.

Grab Bags of Teeth, Claws, and Slime Not all movie creatures are versions of real animals, living or extinct. Some monsters combine body parts. They are nightmare visions of imaginary, terrifying beings. Many of these weird monsters are aliens from other planets.

Alien (1979) introduced one of the most frightening monsters in movie history. Set in the **void** of outer space, astronauts are attacked by an alien with a strange life cycle. In one form, it is a spidery crawler that grabs human faces. It implants an egg that hatches within the victim's body. As an adult, the reptilian alien has an elongated head covered by a hard shell. It also has a layered mouth and rows of razor sharp teeth. *Alien* was also one of the first action films to have a woman hero battle the monster.

Many other movie monsters also go through strange changes. In *Gremlins* (1984), kids were delighted to find a new pet. They were cute little furry creatures. Unfortunately, when gremlins get wet, they turn into nasty creatures with sharp teeth. Bat-wing ears add to their ugly appearance.

Tremors (1989) imagined a family of giant worm-like monsters terrorizing a small Western town. These vicious monsters travel underground at lightning-fast speeds.

The aliens that attack Earth in *Independence Day* (1996) walk on two legs and have two arms. However, they certainly don't look like people. This is partly because they also have slimy tentacles and huge fan-shaped heads.

Starship Troopers (1997) treats an alien invasion like a war movie. Set in the future, Earth's army faces a **severe**

In *Alien,* the monster uses a human victim as a host for its egg.

threat. Instead of soldiers, the human army must fight huge packs of bug-like monsters. Inspired by insects, these aliens have plenty of legs and tough protective armor.

Men in Black (1997) depicts a secret government agency. Its job is to control many different kinds of aliens. Some of them are friendly, like the slim, lizard-like creatures that hang out near the coffeemaker. Others are less welcoming, like the Bugs, which look like gigantic angry cockroaches.

Vocabulary

void (VOYD) *n.* emptiness

severe (suh VEER) *adj.* harsh

The monster movie got another update in *The Host* (2006). A mutant creature grows in the Han River in Seoul, Korea. This slippery, fishy monster attacks hundreds of people. It has many tails and a wide, slimy mouth. One troubled family must band together to fight it. The movie adds a modern fear: the creature may be the host for a deadly virus.

Scare Tactics

No matter what the monster looks like, there are many ways a movie can be scary. Cinematography is the art of photographing and lighting a movie. With the right cinematography, a scary monster can become even scarier.

One trick is to change the focus of the camera. At first, a shape in the background might be blurry because the camera is focused on a person. When the focus suddenly changes, we see that the blur is really a monster!

A jump cut is a sudden shift from one image to another. Jump cuts can increase the suspense. A chase scene might include dozens of jump cuts. These quick shifts make the scene feel more exciting.

The camera's point of view can also change. For example, a camera might change to show what the monster sees. This can be called "monster cam." *Predator* (1987) used a special kind of monster cam. The fierce alien did not see visible light. Instead, it sensed heat. Occasionally, the movie would show what the monster saw: an image of the human body's warmth.

The soundtrack can also exaggerate a fearful mood. Slightly audible groans or scraping sounds can put an audience on edge. A repetitive melody can also increase tension. The two-note theme from *Jaws* is just one example of a soundtrack that arouses shivers and shakes.

Arnold Schwarzenegger was hunted by an invisible alien in *Predator.*

The Power of the Imagination In some cases, film techniques alone can create true terror. *The Blair Witch Project* (1998) is a monster movie without a monster. The film seems like a documentary. The footage shows three young moviemakers lost in the woods. They record their own troubles as they encounter an unseen enemy. The hand-held camera makes the film seem unsteady and nervous. Soon, the audience is imagining a monster much worse than anything a special effects department could create. This film proves that the human imagination really does create the most terrifying monsters of all.

In *The Blair Witch Project,* the young moviemakers are terrorized by an unseen presence for several days. The characters disappear mysteriously, one by one. Only their equipment and the footage they shot is left behind.

Discussion Questions

1. What kind of monster scares you the most? Why?
2. Why do you think monster movies are so popular? Why do people enjoy being frightened?
3. If you were going to invent a new movie monster, what would it look like? Where would it live and how would it behave?
4. Do you think that monster movies reflect our distrust of others? Why or why not?
5. How did people scare themselves before movies were invented?

Face It!

HOW SYMMETRY AND *PHI* AFFECT BEAUTY

MATH

Why do we like to look at certain things? Throughout the ages, people have enjoyed looking at particular buildings, works of art, and even other people. People might say that these buildings, artworks, and other people are beautiful. A familiar expression says that "beauty is in the eye of the beholder," but even critical beholders seem to agree that some people and things are especially good looking. One mathematical idea that seems to **contribute** to our perception of beauty is *symmetry.* An object with symmetry has two sides that have harmony and balance. That is, the two sides have relative positions and the same size and shape.

Vocabulary

contribute (kuhn TRIB yoot) *v.* give or share money, knowledge, or ideas

Christie Brinkley has a very symmetrical face. She is considered to be one of the most beautiful women in the world.

The Beauty of Symmetry

You can find symmetry throughout nature. For example, butterflies and snowflakes are symmetrical. Each **illustrate**s the beauty of the concept.

You can also find symmetry in art and architecture. A gorgeous example of symmetry in architecture is the Taj Mahal. Another example is the Cathedral of Notre Dame.

In the world of manufactured objects, you can find symmetry in everything from iPods to automobiles. For example, NASCAR's Car of Tomorrow has a symmetrical design.

We look for and **respond** to symmetry all around us. In fact, we even look for it in each other. When judging someone's beauty, people unconsciously look for symmetry. What does a symmetrical face look like? It does *not* have one eye that looks droopier than the other. The nose is not crooked. The ears are the same size. Well, that's the idea, anyway.

How Symmetrical Are We?

In the real world, truly symmetrical faces are hard to come by. Simple photography projects **emphasize** the fact that most of us do not have perfectly symmetrical faces. **Focus** on the photographs below. In the first photograph, you see an actual teenager. Nothing in the photograph has been changed.

Now look at the second photograph. Here, the photographer made a mirror image of the left side of the teenager's face. The actual right side of the face has been replaced with this mirror image. How different does it look from the first photograph?

original

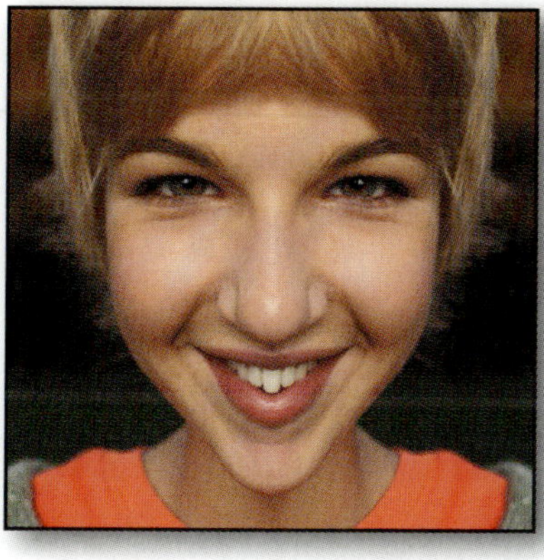

VOCABULARY

illustrate (IL uh STRAYT) *v.* make clear or easily understood by examples

respond (ree SPAHND) *v.* reply or act in answering

emphasize (EM fuh syz) *v.* stress something in order to make it stand out

focus (FOH kuhs) *v.* fix or concentrate on one thing; adjust to make clear

To create the third photograph, the photographer made a mirror image of the *right* side of the teenager's face. Now the left side of the face has been replaced by that mirror image. How different does this photograph look from the first two photographs? How do the changes affect your **reaction** to the teenager?

original

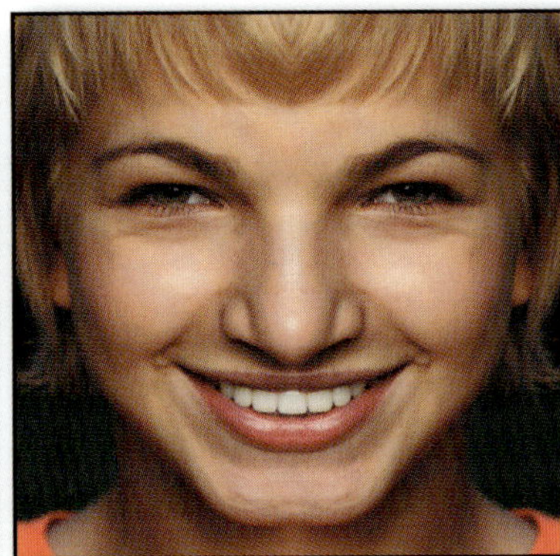

Your Own Symmetry As you can see from the photographs, a lot of us do not have very symmetrical faces. Try this project with your own photograph. Have a friend take a photograph of your face as you look directly at the camera. Then, make two photocopies of the photograph. Use a ruler to find the center of your face, and draw a vertical line to divide each photocopied face into two equal sides. After that, make another photocopy of your face. This time, use the mirror image feature on the photocopier. Again, use a ruler to find the center point on the face, and draw a line down the center. Cut out the left side of this photocopy and place it over one of the original photocopies. Then cut out the right side of the photocopy. Place it on the other original photocopy. Compare these to your original photograph. Do you see any difference?

Symmetry's Attractions

Even though many of us aren't really symmetrical, it turns out that we find people who are symmetrical to be **attractive**. Why should this be? There are a few reasons. First of all, we seem to look for the kind of balance that symmetry provides. For example, you would probably have the urge to straighten a picture that is hanging crooked on a wall.

Vocabulary

reaction (ree AK shuhn) *n.* an opposing action; a response
attractive (uh TRAK tiv) *adj.* pleasing; charming; pretty

We can find another reason in the animal world. Symmetrical animals seem to be healthier than asymmetrical animals. Often, an animal's asymmetry is a sign that it is sick or part of its body is damaged. Symmetrical animals, then, may well produce healthier, stronger offspring. Human beings, like other animals, may unconsciously respond to symmetry as a sign of health and fitness.

An Average Beauty In 1990, psychologists at the University of Arkansas at Fayetteville did an intriguing study using groups of 32 men's photographs and 32 women's photographs. The photographs were digitized, which means that the images were turned into little dots called pixels. Since the photographs could be represented as a matrix of pixel values, the computer could "average" the results. The computer used these results to make one composite, or "average," face. The researchers also made other composite photographs using fewer photographs. They made composites of 4, 8, and 16 faces.

Next, the researchers asked 65 students to look at all of these photographs. The students had to rate how attractive each image was. No one could **dispute** the outcome. The composites of 32 photographs rated higher than any of the photographs of real individuals. In turn, the photographs showing the composites of 16 faces rated higher than the composites of 8 faces.

VOCABULARY

dispute (di SPYOOT) *v.* argue or debate a point; doubt

Piers
Jessica Stam
NAOMI
DRIELLE
JAMISON
NELLY
STEVE MORGAN
ANOUCK
JACQUETTA
Madeleine
Christophe
SIGRID
DACE
RUSLANA
JESSICA
LILLY
JOVITA
Maurine
Nicholas
Shelly

Why would that be? Researchers have different theories. One theory holds that we find the "averaged" faces most attractive because these images are very symmetrical. This is because when many different photographs are blended together, asymmetrical extremes disappear. For example, one photograph might show a woman whose right ear is much larger than her left ear. The composite photograph will not show this asymmetry because of the many different ears in the other women's photographs.

The "averageness" and symmetry of the image in the composite photo may lead us to believe that this person has no genetic mutations. When we look at the composite photograph, we might unconsciously make the **assumption** that this "person" has no serious developmental problems. Therefore, she is probably healthy and strong.

A Beautiful Number

Now that you **appreciate** how important symmetry is, let's look at another mathematical concept that has to do with beauty. That concept is *Phi,* also known as the Golden Mean. This *Phi* is a ratio that seems pleasing to the human eye.

From ancient Greece to modern times, architects and artists all over the world have **persistently** used *Phi* in their designs. The builders of the Grand Mosque in Tunisia used *Phi* in designing the proportions of the minaret.

Artists like Leonardo da Vinci used *Phi* in some of their most famous works. Modern artists like Mondrian used *Phi* in their patterned artwork.

Phi also can be found throughout nature. Here is one lovely example.

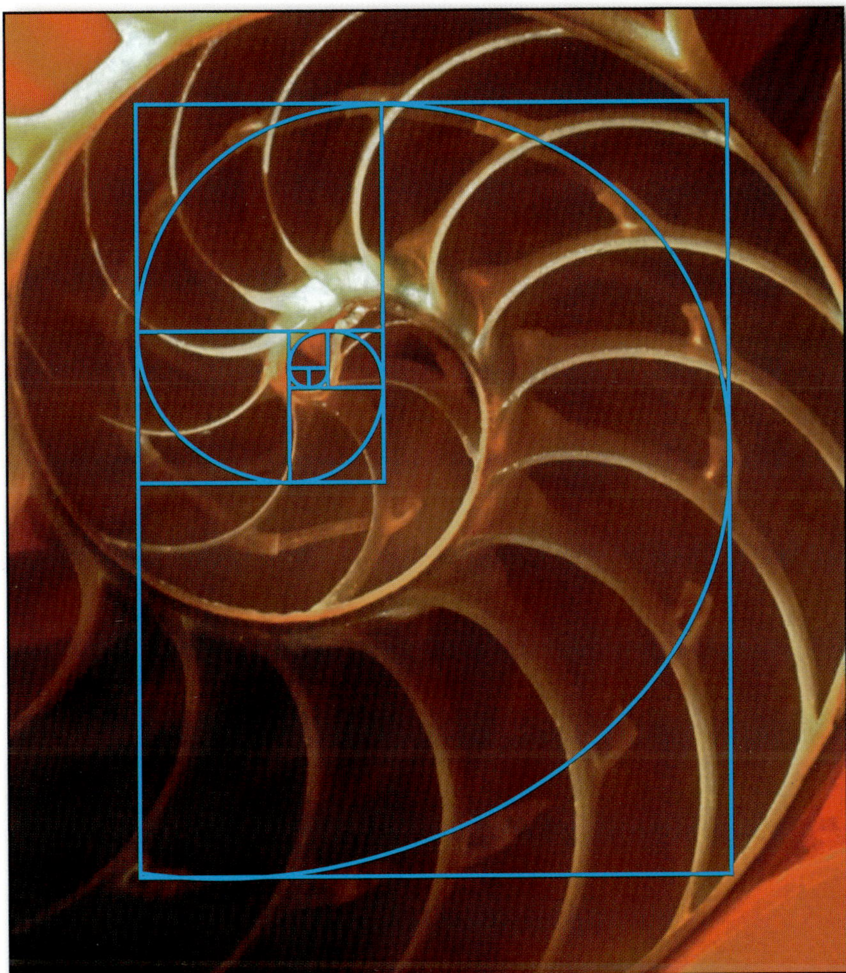

The shell of the chambered nautilus is a symbol of beauty and perfect proportion.

VOCABULARY

assumption (uh SUMP shuhn) *n.* the act of assuming or taking for granted

appreciate (uh PREE shee AYT) *v.* be grateful for; recognize worth of something or someone

persistently (per SIST uhnt lee) *adv.* firmly and steadily

Why *Phi*?

What exactly is *Phi*? *Phi,* also known as the Golden Ratio, is represented as 1.618. Let's look at two lines to **define** *Phi* more clearly. The first line is Line AB.

Now, multiply the length of the first line by 1.618. The result is the length of the second line, Line AC.

If you compare the length of the red line, AC, to the length of the blue line, AB, you have *Phi.* If you compare the length of the blue line, AB, to the length of the section of the red line that starts where the blue line ends, BC, you have *Phi.*

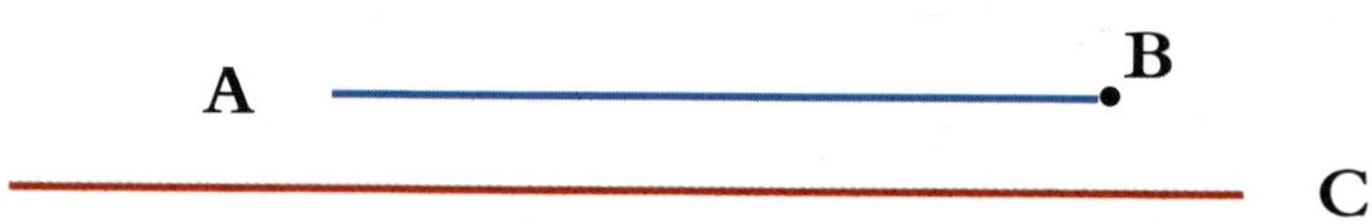

You can find many geometric shapes that exhibit *Phi.* Below, these lines make what's called a Golden Rectangle.

The lines can be combined to make other shapes, as well.

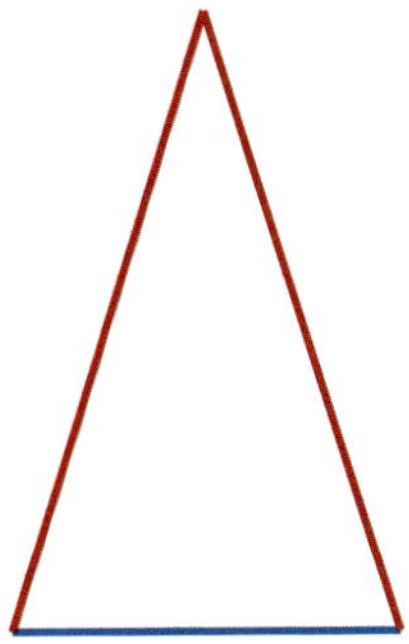

The Anatomy of *Phi* Strangely enough, this golden ratio can even be found in us. In the human body, many claim that you can see *Phi* when you measure the length of the head and compare it to the distance from the top of the head to the navel. *Phi* lovers think that you can also find it in the lengths of the bones of the fingers. They claim that it is also in the length of the hand compared to the length of the forearm.

Actually, it's probably impossible for one person to have precise *Phi* measurements in all these areas. However, here's the thing. Just as some **conclude** that those who are most symmetrical are the most attractive, others conclude that the closer a person's body is to actually embodying these *Phi* ratios, the more attractive that person is!

Vocabulary

define (dee FYN) *v.* set clear boundaries or distinct characteristics

conclude (kuhn KLOOD) *v.* form an opinion based on evidence

Phi in Your Face

That brings us to the human face. While much has been written to **establish** the importance of *Phi* in the human body, even more has been written about *Phi* in our facial features. Here are some of the *Phi*ndings.

- The head makes a golden rectangle.
- If you compare a) the distance of the eyes to the chin to b) the distance of the mouth to the chin, you find *Phi*.
- Our front teeth make a golden rectangle. When you compare the width to the length of the teeth, you find *Phi*.

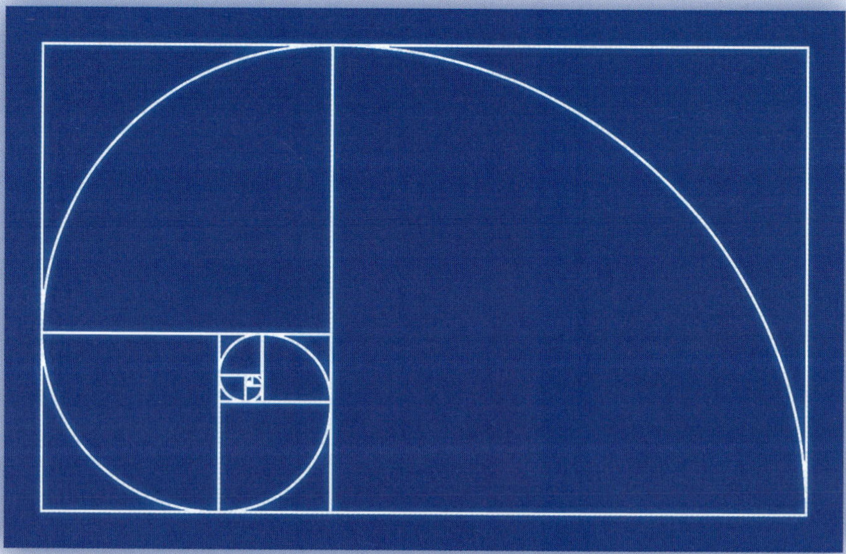

The Fibonacci spiral resembles the shape of a chambered nautilus shell.

In the past few years, a former plastic surgeon, Dr. Stephen Marquardt, has gained media attention for his theories on beauty. Marquardt has studied the **characteristics** of beautiful faces in art throughout the ages. What do these faces have that never fails to **impress** the viewer? Using *Phi* as a building block, Marquardt has devised a mask that he believes represents the ideal in beauty. In his research, he superimposed the mask over photos of sketches, paintings, and photographs. By doing this, he says he learned that those people whose faces **conveyed** *Phi,* as shown in the mask, were the most attractive.

According to Marquardt, the more attractive a person is, the more likely it is that the mask will "fit." Marquardt claims that this is true regardless of the individual's ethnic background. These findings present a **conflict** with the theory that a person's idea of beauty depends on when and where that person is living. Marquardt, however, believes that no matter what era or country a person is from, he or she will respond to the beauty of well-proportioned features, as illustrated on his *Phi* mask.

Vocabulary

establish (uh STAB lish) *v.* determine; make sure of; set up

characteristic (KAR uhk tuhr IS tik) *n.* a quality that makes something recognizable

impress (im PRES) *v.* make someone feel admiration and respect; make clear the importance of something

conveyed (kuhn VAYD) *v.* made known; expressed

conflict (KAHN flikt) *n.* opposition between or among different forces; clash

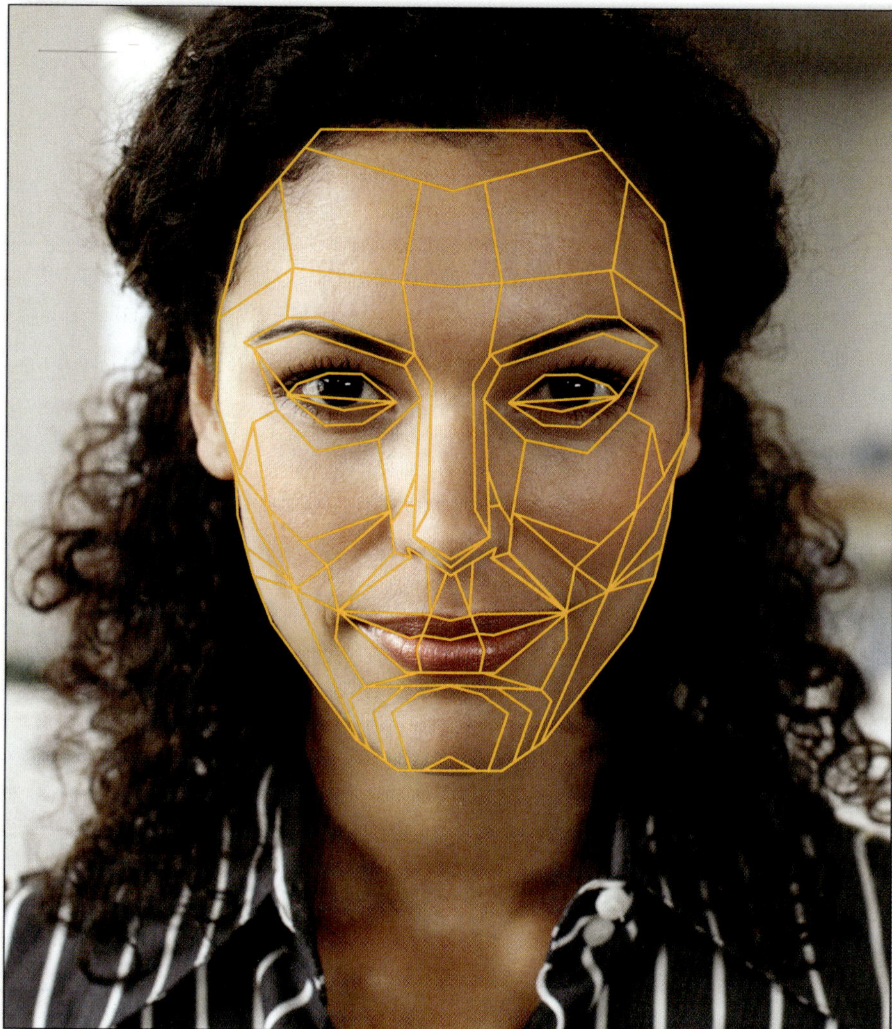

Do you think this young woman is beautiful?
How closely does her face "fit" the mask?

And what if an individual does not "fit" the mask? Can a less attractive person **acquire** *Phi* proportions? On his website, Marquardt shows examples of women who use makeup to bring their features closer to the ideal. Given his profession, of course, Marquardt also advocates surgery as a **practical** step toward reaching this ideal.

Beauty's Tricks

Many of us admire beautiful models and movie stars. Many of us are attracted to attractive people. Where is the harm in that? All this could seem unimportant, except for the findings on how beauty affects our judgments about other people. Researchers have found in study after study that we tend to think "beauty is good." The studies work this way. Researchers show subjects photographs of strangers. The people rated as being the most attractive are also rated as being the nicest, the most successful, the most reliable, and the most confident.

You can imagine the **potential** for **bias** in all kinds of cases that **involve** these kinds of judgments. Does a better-looking person have more **suitors**? Yes. Is a better-looking employee more likely to get a raise? Yes. Is a better-looking defendant more likely to be acquitted by a jury? Yes. Is a better-looking toddler more likely to be buckled in a shopping cart? Remarkably, yes again.

Still, it's important to remember that these beautiful people are *not really* smarter or better than the rest of us, even if they may have more confidence. In a recent

Vocabulary

acquire (uh KWYR) *v.* gain possession of

practical (PRAK ti kuhl) *adj.* level-headed; efficient; realistic

potential (poh TEN shuhl) *n.* possibility; capability

bias (BY uhs) *n.* an opinion about whether a person, group, or idea is good or bad that influences how you deal with it

involve (in VAHLV) *v.* include in an activity, discussion, or task; make complicated

suitors (SOOT erz) *n.* men who court a woman or seek to marry her

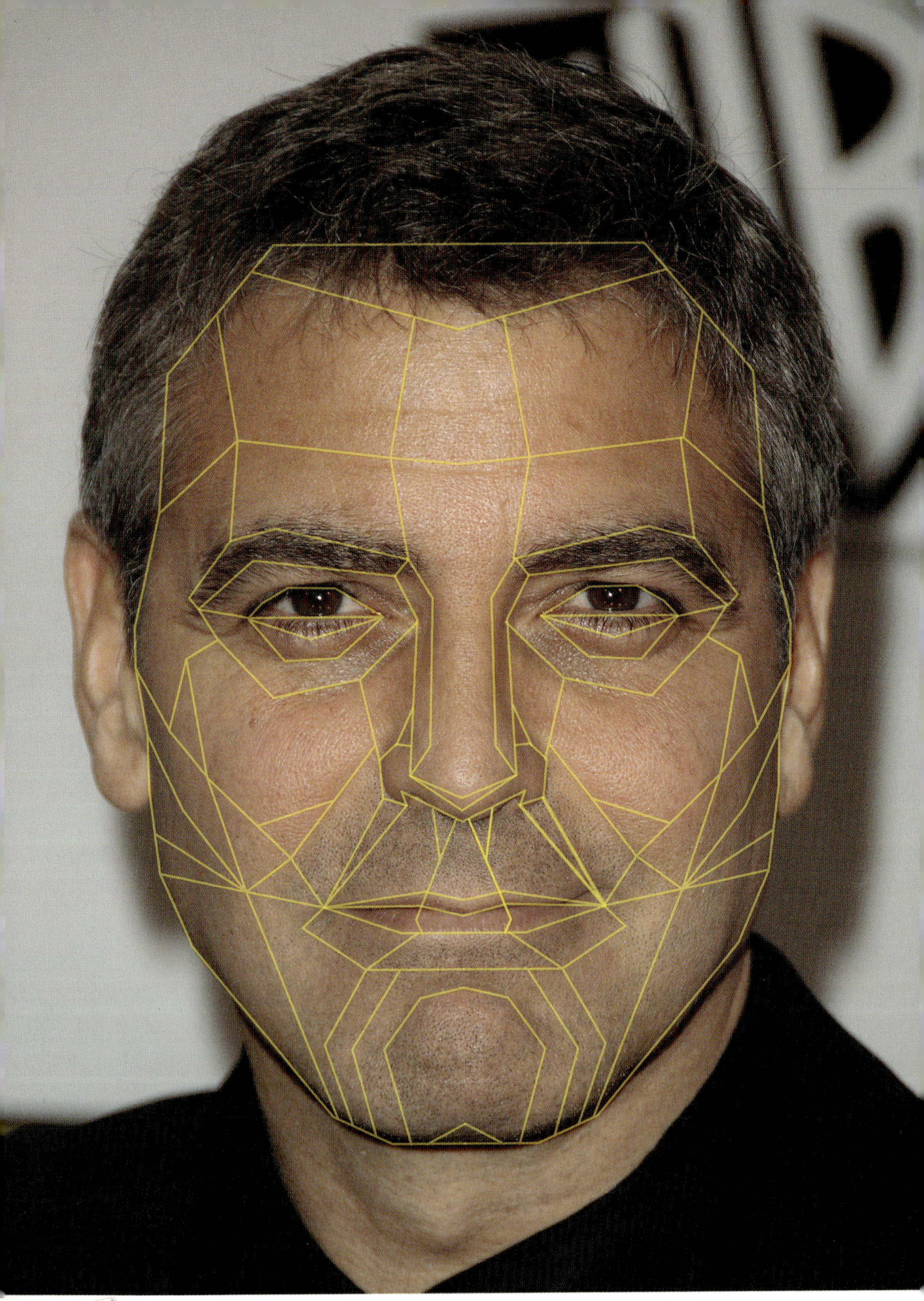

Actor George Clooney has been called one of the most beautiful men.

study, researchers gave college and graduate students mazes to solve. Before they started their task, researchers asked the students how they thought they would do. The attractive students felt more positive about their abilities. As it turned out, they did no better than anyone else.

So, when thinking about your reaction to other people, remember that you can easily make the mistake of overrating beauty. Even though you may not be able to control your response to a symmetrical, *Phi*ne-looking face, you *can* control what you do about it.

Discussion Questions

1. Why do you think that many people go to great lengths to change their **appearance**?

2. How does beauty affect your decisions about other people?

3. What other factors besides facial symmetry and proportion might enter into your immediate reaction to someone new?

Vocabulary

appearance (uh PER uhns) *n.* the look of a person or thing

Glossary

acquire (uh KWYR) *v.* gain possession of **8, 32, 72**

appearance (uh PER uhns) *n.* the look of a person or thing **75**

appreciate (uh PREE shee AYT) *v.* be grateful for; recognize worth of something or someone **8, 23, 66**

arouse (uh ROWZ) *v.* awaken one's attention or interest; stir into action **16, 30, 45**

assumption (uh SUMP shuhn) *n.* the act of assuming or taking for granted **35, 66**

astonish (uh STON ish) *v.* amaze **30, 41**

attractive (uh TRAK tiv) *adj.* pleasing; charming; pretty **63**

audible (AW duh buhl) *adj.* loud enough to be heard **51**

benevolence (buh NEV uh luhns) *n.* kindliness **15**

bias (BY uhs) *n.* an opinion about whether a person, group, or idea is good or bad that influences how you deal with it **73**

characteristic (KAR uhk tuhr IS tik) *n.* a quality that makes something recognizable **15, 32, 51, 71**

chronological (KRAHN uh LAHJ I kuhl) *adj.* arranged in the order in which events occur **51**

compulsion (kuhm PUL shuhn) *n.* a driving, irresistible force **7, 42**

conceited (kuhn SEET id) *adj.* having a very high opinion of oneself **10**

conclude (kuhn KLOOD) *v.* form an opinion based on evidence **35, 69**

conflict (KAHN flikt) *n.* opposition between or among different forces; clash **14, 45, 71**

contribute (kuhn TRIB yoot) *v.* give or share money, knowledge, or ideas **5, 30, 59**

conveyed (kuhn VAYD) *v.* made known; expressed **43, 71**

critique (kri TEEK) *n.* an assessment or critical analysis, usually of a creative or literary work **19**

defiant (dee FY uhnt) *adj.* boldly resisting **44**

define (dee FYN) *v.* set clear boundaries or distinct characteristics **11, 29, 45, 68**

destitute (DES tuh toot) *adj.* living in complete poverty **6**

dispute (di SPYOOT) *v.* argue or debate a point; doubt **64**

emphasize (EM fuh syz) *v.* stress something in order to make it stand out **14, 37, 42, 61**

establish (uh STAB lish) *v.* determine; make sure of; set up **32, 51, 70**

focus (FOH kuhs) *v.* to fix or concentrate on one thing; adjust to make clear **5, 25, 42, 61**

identify (eye DEN tuh fy) *v.* recognize something or discover exactly what it is **47**

ignore (ig NOHR) *v.* pay no attention to; refuse to consider; disregard **11, 44**

illusion (i LOO zhun) *n.* an unreal, deceptive, or misleading appearance or image **22**

illustrate (IL uh STRAYT) *v.* make clear or easily understood by examples **16, 28, 60**

image (IM ij) *n.* picture **27**

impress (im PRES) *v.* make someone feel admiration and respect; make clear the importance of something **71**

involve (in VAHLV) *v.* include in an activity, discussion, or task; make complicated **33, 41, 73**

involvement (in VAHLV muhnt) *n.* participation **12, 25**

meager (MEE ger) *adj.* of poor quality; small amount **37**

metamorphosis (MET uh MOHR fuh sis) *n.* change of form **42**

perception (puhr SEP shuhn) *n.* ability to see **29**

persistently (per SIST uhnt lee) *adv.* firmly and steadily **66**

perspective (puhr SPEK tiv) *n.* a specific point of view in understanding or judging things **6**

potential (poh TEN shuhl) *n.* possibility; capability **5, 73**

potential (poh TEN shuhl) *adj.* possible; that can, but has not yet, come into being **25**

practical (PRAK ti kuhl) *adj.* level-headed; efficient; realistic **11, 72**

pride (PRYD) *n.* proper respect for yourself; sense of your own dignity or worth; self-respect **15**

reaction (ree AK shuhn) *n.* an opposing action; a response **6, 32, 41, 62**

reflect (ri FLEKT) *v.* express; show **40**

respond (ree SPAHND) *v.* to reply or act in answering **19, 25, 44, 60**

sequence (SEE kwuhns) *n.* one thing after another in logical or chronological order **26, 42**

severe (suh VEER) *adj.* harsh **52**

sluggishly (SLUG ish lee) *adv.* as if lacking energy **35**

snuffs (SNUFS) *v.* extinguishes; puts out **51**

suitors (SOOT erz) *n.* men who court a woman or seek to marry her **73**

summarize (SUM uh RYZ) *v.* briefly state the most important events in a story **10, 26**

void (VOYD) *n.* emptiness **11, 52**

Photo Credits

Cover: © Getty Images; **4–5:** © Rungroj Yongrit/epa/Corbis; **6–7:** "Prince Siddharta meets a priest who presuades him to become a monk, episode from the 'Kwakogenzaiingakyo', illustration from 'Kokka', March 1924 (colour litho) by Chinese School (20th century) © Bibliotheque des Arts Decoratifs, Paris, France/Archives Charmet/The Bridgeman Art Library"; **8–9:** © The Art Archive/Musée d'Orsay Paris/Dagli Orti; **10:** © Zen Shui Photography/Veer; **12–13:** © Jeremy Horner/Corbis; **13:** © Panoramic Images/Getty Images; **14:** © Snark/Art Resource, NY; **16:** "Portrait of the Empress Wu Zetian (625-705) (gouache on paper) by Chinese School © Musee Guimet, Paris, France/Archives Charmet/The Bridgeman Art Library"; **18–19:** © JTB Photo Communications, Inc./Alamy; **20:** © Werner Forman/Art Resource, NY; **22–23: t.** © Marvin Newman/Getty Images; **22: m.** © Raul Gonzalez Perez/Photo Researchers, Inc.; **22–23: b.** Sunday Afternoon on the Island of La Grande Jatte, 1884-86 (oil on canvas) by Georges Pierre Seurat (1859-91) © Art Institute of Chicago, IL, USA/The Bridgeman Art Library; **23:** © Visuals Unlimited/Corbis; **24:** © Visuals Unlimited/Corbis; **26–27:** © Scott Barrow/Veer/Corbis; **27:** © L Birmingham/Custom Medical Stock Photo; **28:** © Eaton/Custom Medical Stock Photo; **28–29:** © VisionsofAmerica/Joe Sohm/Getty Images; **30–31:** © Omikron/Photo Researchers, Inc.; **33: l.** © ISM/Phototake — All rights reserved.; **33: r.** © ISM/Phototake — All rights reserved.; **34:** © Swim Ink 2, LLC/CORBIS; **35:** © Art Resource, NY; **36–37:** © Art Resource, NY; **38:** © Jim Craigmyle/Corbis; **40–41:** © Randy Faris/Corbis; **42–43:** © UNIVERSAL/THE KOBAL COLLECTION; **44:** © UNIVERSAL/THE KOBAL COLLECTION; **46:** © ALLIED ARTISTS/THE KOBAL COLLECTION; **46–47:** © PARAMOUNT/DREAMWORKS/THE KOBAL COLLECTION; **48–49:** © UNIVERSAL/THE KOBAL COLLECTION; **50–51:** © TOHO/THE KOBAL COLLECTION; **52–53:** © 20TH CENTURY FOX/THE KOBAL COLLECTION/PENN, ROBERT; **54–55:** © 20TH CENTURY FOX/THE KOBAL COLLECTION/ROSENTHAL, ZADE; **56:** © ARTISAN PICS/THE KOBAL COLLECTION; **56–57:** © ARTISAN PICS/THE KOBAL COLLECTION; **58–59:** © Evan Agostini/Getty Images; **60–61:** © Sabine Lubenow/Jupiter Images; **61–62:** © STOCK 4B/Getty Images; **63:** © Simon Watson/Getty Images; **64–65:** © Scott Gries/Getty Images; **67:** © Dan McCoy/Science Faction Images; **70:** © SEYMOUR/Photo Researchers, Inc.; **72:** © C. Devan/zefa/Corbis; **74–75:** © Frank Trapper/Corbis